Early
Reader

A Gift For

From

How to Use Your Interactive Story Buddy™:

1. Activate your Story Buddy™ by pressing the "On / Off" button on the ear.
2. Read the story aloud in a quiet place. Speak in a clear voice when you see the highlighted phrases.
3. Listen to your Story Buddy™ respond with several different phrases throughout the book.

Clarity and speed of reading affect the way Jingle™ responds. He may not always respond to young children.

Watch for even more Interactive Story Buddy™ characters.

For more information, visit us on the Web at Hallmark.com/StoryBuddy.

Set Builder: Randy Stewart
Photo Retoucher: Jeff Jones
Project Coordinator: Kerry Ramirez
Photographer: Jake Johnson
Storyboard & Character Development: Karla Taylor
Character & Prop Designers: Ken Crow, Ruth Donikowski, Rich Gilson, and Susan Tague

ISBN: 978-1-59530-277-9

XKT1085

Printed and bound in China
MARI2

Copyright © 2010 Hallmark Licensing, LLC
Published by Hallmark Gift Books, a division of Hallmark Cards, Inc., Kansas City, MO 64141
Visit us on the Web at Hallmark.com.

Editors: Megan Langford and Theresa Trinder
Art Director: Kevin Swanson
Designer: Mary Eakin
Production Artist: Dan Horton
Photo Stylist: Betsy Gantt Stewart

I Reply TECHNOLOGY™

Hallmark's **I Reply Technology** brings your Story Buddy™ to life! When you read the key phrases out loud, your Story Buddy™ gives a variety of responses, so each time you read feels as magical as the first.

Jingle All the Way

BOOK 1

By Tom Shay-Zapien

Hallmark
GIFT BOOKS

There are lots of stories about good little boys and girls—
but there aren't many stories about good little dogs.
But this is a story about Jingle the husky pup.
And Jingle was a good dog.

He never made a mess. He never chewed holes in things. He never (not even once) kept people awake at night with his barking. And he always—OK, *almost* always—did what he was told.

NO DOGS ALLOWED!

One day, Jingle was resting beside the front steps of Pineville Elementary School. Suddenly, the school bell began clanging out loud. And the children who were *inside* ran *outside*. That made Jingle very happy.

So he came back the next day. And the same thing happened!

The bell rang and the children hurried out. It was amazing!

Kevin patted his belly.

Sarah scratched his ears.

Jennifer said, "Jingle, you're a good dog!"

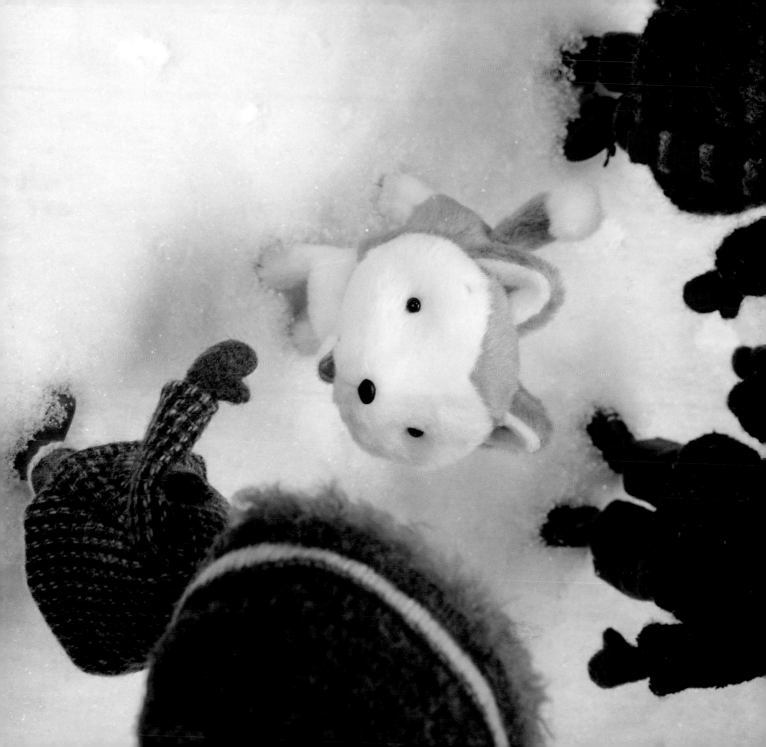

Jingle loved to bark hello.
Jingle even loved to sing.

But what Jingle loved most was being with his friends. He liked to race Kevin to the edge of the schoolyard. But every day, Kevin said,

"Bye, Jingle! It's time for me to go!"

Sometimes he followed Sarah to the school bus. But Sarah only said,
"Sorry, Jingle! I've gotta go home!"

One snowy day, Jingle even dashed all the way to Jennifer's house. Jennifer laughed. "Silly dog! Jingle, you've gotta go home!"

CLOSED for the HOLIDAYS

Usually, Jingle did exactly what he was told. But since he didn't have a home, he couldn't go there.

Instead, he went back to Pineville Elementary and waited for the school bell. He waited all night and all day, but it didn't ring.

Jingle decided to look for his friends. After all, they were the closest thing he had to a family. He searched everywhere—but the kids were nowhere to be found.

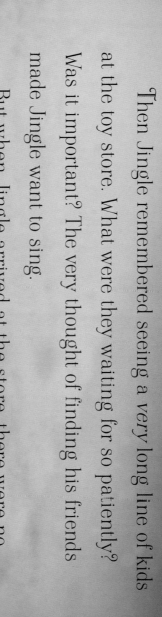

Then Jingle remembered seeing a very long line of kids at the toy store. What were they waiting for so patiently? Was it important? The very thought of finding his friends made Jingle want to sing.

But when Jingle arrived at the store, there were no children. There was only a colorful storefront window and a whole lot of quiet.

Jingle was tired from all his searching, so he made his way behind the toy store and plopped into the first soft place he found and fell fast asleep. And even though it didn't feel like a home, it was quite cozy.

Moments later, someone carefully lifted the bag Jingle had snuggled into. "Well, what have we here?" a voice spoke warmly. "Someone all alone? At Christmas?"

Placing the green velveteen bag in the front of his sled, the man remembered a letter he'd been given earlier that day from a good little boy in the toy store. "Ho-ho-ho!" he said to himself. "This gives me an idea!"

He wasn't sure what was going to happen, but suddenly Jingle felt very happy.

The next morning Jingle was surrounded by the smell of pine and peppermint. There was a fancy collar around his neck with a bell that jingled whenever he moved.

But the best surprise of all came when Jingle saw Andrew, one of his friends from school.

"It's Jingle!" Andrew said. "Jingle, you're such a good dog!"

The two friends spent the rest of Christmas Day playing together, Jingle's bell ringing merrily all the while. That night, before Andrew turned out the lights in his room, Jingle hopped onto the bed. Andrew said, "Jingle, stay!" And Jingle did.

Did you have fun with Jingle?
We would love to hear from you!

Please send your comments to:
Hallmark Book Feedback
P.O. Box 419034
Mail Drop 215
Kansas City, MO 64141

Or e-mail us at:
booknotes@hallmark.com